MIAMI MEMORIES
A Midcentury Journey

Mary L. Martin • Tina Skinner • Nathaniel Wolfgang-Price

Schiffer Publishing Ltd®

4880 Lower Valley Road, Atglen, PA 19310 USA

Library of Congress Cataloging-in-Publication Data:

Martin, Mary L., 1936-
  Miami memories : a midcentury journey / by Mary L. Martin, Tina Skinner,
Nathaniel Wolfgang-Price.
     p. cm.
  ISBN 0-7643-2176-5 (pbk.)
1. Miami (Fla.)—History—20th century—Pictorial works. 2. Miami (Fla.)—
Buildings, structures, etc.—Pictorial works. 3. Historic buildings—Florida—
Miami—Pictorial works. 4. Miami (Fla.)—Social life and customs—20th cen-
tury—Pictorial works. I. Skinner, Tina. II. Wolfgang-Price, Nathaniel. III. Title.

F319.M6M29 2005
975.9'381'0630222—dc22
                              2004021318

Designed by John P. Cheek
Cover design by John P. Cheek
Type set in Grenadier/Aldine 721 BT

ISBN: 0-7643-2176-5
Printed in China

Published by Schiffer Publishing Ltd.
4880 Lower Valley Road
Atglen, PA 19310
Phone: (610) 593-1777; Fax: (610) 593-2002
E-mail: Info@schifferbooks.com

For the largest selection of fine reference books on this and related subjects, please visit our web site at **www.schifferbooks.com**
We are always looking for people to write books on new and related
subjects. If you have an idea for a book please contact us at the above
address.

This book may be purchased from the publisher.
Include $3.95 for shipping.
Please try your bookstore first.
You may write for a free catalog.

In Europe, Schiffer books are distributed by
Bushwood Books
6 Marksbury Ave.
Kew Gardens
Surrey TW9 4JF England
Phone: 44 (0) 20 8392-8585; Fax: 44 (0) 20 8392-9876
E-mail: info@bushwoodbooks.co.uk
Free postage in the U.K., Europe; air mail at cost.

TABLE OF CONTENTS

Miami: A Short History of the Resort

Miami's early fortunes were generally delivered to the small villagers and homesteaders in the form of salvaged wealth from the wreckage from ships run afoul on the coastal reefs. All that changed when railroad magnate Henry M. Flagler set his sights down the east Florida coast. His first train arrived in Miami on April 13, 1896, and a year later guests were flocking to his 400-room, Royal Palm Hotel, including such notables as Andrew Carnegie, the Vanderbilt family, and John D. Rockefeller. The rest of the nation followed.

By 1910, the population and the number of new businesses were exploding. Indiana millionaire Carl Fisher was one of many entrepreneurs to capitalize on the tourist potential of Miami Beach, building hotels, golf courses, and polo fields. The beautiful beaches, opulent hotels, and racetracks attracted a large number of well-to-do visitors.

The Florida land boom drew thousands of people from all over America in the 1920s, all hoping to "strike it rich" in real estate. One enamored newspaper writer wrote in 1928 that Miami by the Sea was "the most gorgeous example of upper-class civilization on the planet."

The Great Depression and World War II offered brief setbacks, followed by a post-war boom that ushered in a "Golden Age" that lasted well into the 1950s for Miami. Built mostly between 1933 and 1949, the South Beach Art Deco district is an architectural showcase of nearly 1000 historic buildings, placed on the National Register of Historic Places in 1979.

This mix of historic buildings includes both Tropical Deco and the MiMo styles claimed as unique to the region. Notable architects accepted the many commissions generated by the region's building booms. Their "Tropical Deco" work was fueled by a world-wide passion for Art Deco or "streamlined" architecture, married to the local inspirations of warm resort elements including Spanish Colonial influences, motifs from Aztec and Native American cultures, nautical elements like porthole windows, and tropical imagery like flamingos and palm trees. Following World War II, a fresh profusion of resort architecture sprung up throughout the resort area. Nicknamed MiMo today, the Miami Modern style is embodied in hotels, diners, restaurants, and other landmarks that were added to the architectural legacy of the city.

The popularity of rail travel waned, but Miami still enjoyed an influx of tourists. The Golden Age of the automobile was underway, with American families setting out to explore in their comfy sedans. By sea, American and European passenger lines adopted Miami as both a destination and as a starting point for journeys further south to places like Cuba or the Bahamas. Today Miami hosts one of the largest collection of cruise ships in the world. Privately owned yachts would also sail down to Miami and anchor in the shelter of Biscayne Bay during the winter season. In 1935, air travel became available as Eastern Airlines connected Miami with Chicago, New York, and all points in between, and Pan American Airways offered flights between Miami and Central and South American destinations.

Sport fishing, water sports, horse and greyhound racing, and more exotic attractions like the many orange groves, the Everglades, and Parrot Jungle and Monkey Jungle beckoned. Before long, Miami had earned the reputation of "America's Winter Playground." The city has promoted itself alternately as "The Convention City," "The City of Happiness," and "Outdoor Sports Capital of America."

Today Miami Beach has a reputation worldwide as party town to the rich and famous. By day it is populated by sunbathers stretched out poolside or in the sand, as well as super models who alight here for swimsuit photo shoots. By night, the neon-lit beachside resort rocks well into the wee hours. There is still something for everyone here – luxury hotels, tropical waters, and a wide variety of attractions.

For those who have been coming for years, or for first-timers looking for a little history, this book offers a colorful romp back in time, to a Miami of yesterday.

"Greetings from Miami."

Many servicemen stationed in Miami sent home postcards like this one.

Sand IN MY SHOES

MIAMI

Magic city by the sea,
Made for mirth and gaiety;

In the sunshine of your smile,
Is a charm that can beguile

All our care and worriment,
And dispel our discontent;

Mecca of the free outdoors,
Millions journey to your shores;

If your sand gets in one shoe,
It will bring them back to you.

LETHA MADDEN

© CURT TEICH & CO., INC.

Tourists captivated by Miami's beauty developed "sand in their shoes," which meant they would want to return to Miami.

Edgar Leslie and Joseph Burke wrote "Moon Over Miami" in 1935; the song was later featured in a movie by the same name starring Betty Grable.

D. C. 135—"Off to Study," Army Air Forces Technical Training Command, Miami Beach, Fla.

During World Wars I and II, pilots received basic training at the Army Air Force Technical Training Command in Miami Beach.

Miami was a popular port-of-call for cruise lines traveling from Europe and the continental United States.

This globe, in the lobby of the Pan American Airways Terminal in the Miami Airport, was oriented so that Miami would be on top of the globe every two minutes.

Travelling through the Orange Groves, Florida

Tourists take a train ride through one of Miami's many orange groves.

F.E.C. Streamliner
"The Champion"
at Miami

The Florida East Coast Railway steamer, "The Champion." The first train came to Miami on April 13, 1896.

City Overviews

Aerial Shots

From the Air, Miami Beach, Florida   363

An aerial view of the Dade County Causeway, which connects Miami with Miami Beach.

59   Hotel Row, Overlooking Bayfront Park, Miami, Florida

17,231

An aerial view of Bayfront Park and the hotels on Biscayne Boulevard.

D.C. 242— "The Magic City," Miami, Fla.

"The Magic City" of Miami.

A few of the many hotels located
on Biscayne Boulevard.

D77:-SKYSCRAPER HOTELS ON BISCAYNE BOULEVARD,
MIAMI, FLORIDA

Because of the large number of tourists that visited regularly, Miami Beach was known as "The Nation's Playground."

M.32—Ocean Front Hotels, "The Nation's Playground," Miami Beach, Florida

Bayfront Park with the Municipal Auditorium in the foreground.

DC-169—Beautiful Miami — "The Nation's Playground"

PHOTO BY CITY OF MIAMI NEWS BUREAU

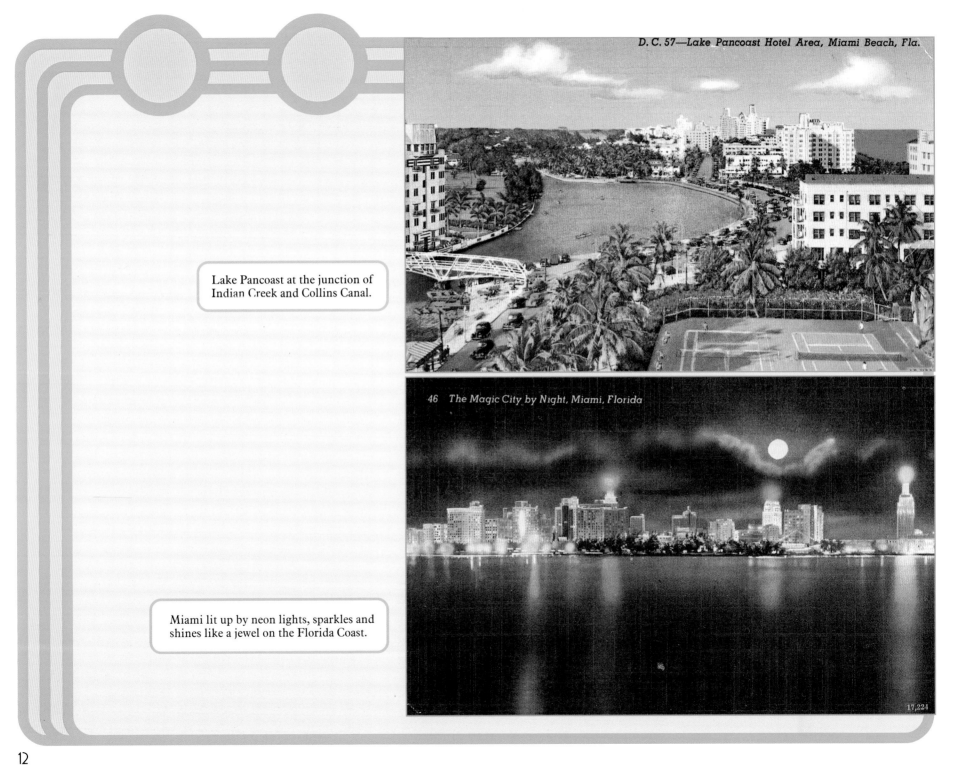

D. C. 57—Lake Pancoast Hotel Area, Miami Beach, Fla.

Lake Pancoast at the junction of Indian Creek and Collins Canal.

46   The Magic City by Night, Miami, Florida

Miami lit up by neon lights, sparkles and shines like a jewel on the Florida Coast.

MOON OVER MIAMI, MIAMI, FLORIDA   21

Miami framed by the prow and rigging of a wooden sailing ship like the ones that brought the first non-native settlers to Miami from the Bahamas in the early 1800s.

13

Ocean Drive in Miami Beach, the location of Lummus Park and Public Beach.

EDITH & FRITZ RESTAURANT, 3236 NORTH MIAMI AVE., MIAMI 37, FLORIDA

Washington Avenue was known as the center of shopping in Miami Beach.

DC-80—Palms on Biscayne Blvd., Miami, Fla.

Palms line both sides of Biscayne Boulevard.

Flagler Street is named after Henry Flagler, who was instrumental in the early development of Miami as a city.

DC-124—Miami and Flagler Streets
One of Miami's Busy Intersections

The five-story Burdines Department Store, built around 1910, became Miami's first "skyscraper."

Home to the constantly changing parade of tourists, the majority of hotels on Collins Avenue were built in an Art Deco style that could be seen throughout the city.

Running the entire length of Miami Beach, Collins Avenue is home to many of the city's hotels. The avenue was considered the fashionable place to stay by many of the upper-class tourists who visited Miami Beach.

Hotel Row, Collins Avenue, Miami Beach, Fla.

The Shelborne, Raleigh, Grossinger, and National hotels on Collins Avenue.

234   A Fantasy in Neon, Collins Ave., Miami Beach

The Raleigh, the Ritz-Plaza, the National, the Sands, and the New Yorker lit up in a "fantasy in neon."

The National, the Grossinger, the Raliegh, and the Shelborne hotels along Collins Avenue.

D. C. 71—Palatial Ocean Front Hotels, Miami Beach, Fla.

D. C. 65—Exclusive Hotels on Collins Avenue, Miami Beach, Fla.

The Embassy, the Monroe Towers, and the Sea Isle Hotels, on Collins Avenue.

D.C. 123—Collins Ave., Looking North from 19th St., Miami Beach, Fla.

PHOTO BY VERNE O. WILLIAMS   Showing Town House, Dempsey-Vanderbilt and Roney Plaza Hotels

The Town House, Dempsey-Vanderbilt, and Roney Plaza Hotels, three more of the exclusive hotels located on Collins Avenue.

Collins Avenue was nicknamed Hotel Row because of the sheer number of hotels located there.

DC-222—Luxurious Hotel Row
Looking South on Collins Avenue
Miami Beach, Florida

Looking South from 17th and Collins Ave.,
Miami Beach, Fla.   415

A view of Collins Avenue looking from the corner of 17th Street.

Lincoln Road was known as one of the most exclusive shopping areas in America.

D. C. 75—"Lincoln Road," America's Most Famous, Exclusive Shopping Area, Miami Beach, Fla.

Lincoln Road as seen from Washington Avenue, another of Miami Beach's "exclusive" areas.

M.149—Lincoln Road at Night
Miami Beach, Florida

When the sun went down, many tourists would migrate from the beaches to the shops on Lincoln Road.

There were many stores on Lincoln Road ranging from the fashionable Burdine's Department Store to Woolworths.

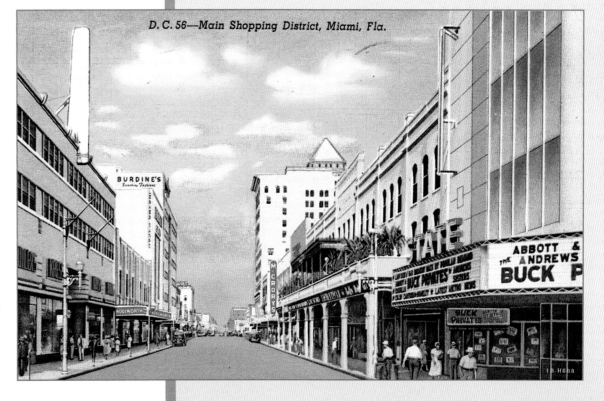

D.C. 56—Main Shopping District, Miami, Fla.

The Miami Beach Federal Savings and Loan Association was the second federal savings association formed in the United States.

D. C. 62—Lincoln Road and Washington Avenue Business Section, Miami Beach, Fla.

IB-H894

Lincoln Road, Miami Beach, Florida   258

Designers would often premier their collections in shops on Lincoln Road. A shopper could see "today what America will wear next summer."

Cars wait while a boat passes under the causeway that connects Miami with Miami Beach.

Bird's-Eye View, Venetian and County Causeways, Miami Beach, Florida 334

The Venetian and County Causeways. The Venetian Causeway was built in 1925. Its most prominent feature is the "X" shaped pattern in the middle of the guardrails.

The Bahia Honda Bridge is the highest part of the highway that connects Miami with the Florida Keys.

D. C. 33——Forty-First Street Bridge over Indian Creek
Miami Beach, Fla.

One of the bridges that span Indian Creek in Miami Beach, this one connects Forty-First Street on both sides of the Creek.

SUNKEN GARDENS, HARVEY FIRESTONE ESTATE, MIAMI BEACH, FLORIDA—KM15

The sunken gardens at the Harvey Firestone Estate are typical of those found throughout Miami.

Ocean Drive, Lummus Park, and Hotels, Miami Beach, Fla.   404

Lummus Park and Ocean Drive, Miami Beach.

Lummus Park was opened in 1909 and is a popular destination for tourists and natives alike.

An aerial view of Lummus Park in front of Downtown Miami.

The Wm. Jennings Bryan Memorial was built from 1925-1928 and is one of the few early religious buildings in Miami that was designed to be handicapped accessible in order to accommodate Bryan's wife, who was confined to a wheelchair.

17,807 Flamingo Park, Miami Beach, Florida 242

The central walkway in Miami Beach's Flamingo Park.

A thatched Tahitian hut does not seem out of place in the tropical setting of Miami's Bayfront Park.

5 Bayfront Park and Skyline, Miami, Florida

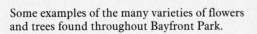

15089

An aerial view of Bayfront Park, a showplace of tropical landscaping that attracts thousands of visitors every year.

Some examples of the many varieties of flowers and trees found throughout Bayfront Park.

D. C. 69—View of Bayfront Park at Foot of Flagler Street, Miami, Fla.

IB-H901

BISCAYNE BAY AS SEEN FROM BAYFRONT PARK, MIAMI, FLORIDA 24

PHOTO BY R. E. SIMPS

Visitors to Bayfront Park in the late 1940s pause
to watch the boats sailing in Biscayne Bay.

AFTERNOON CONCERT IN BAYFRONT PARK BANDSHELL, MIAMI, FLORIDA

3

PHOTO BY G. W. ROMER

Visitors also came to Bayfront in order to hear free concerts
given at the Bandshell, offered daily to the public.

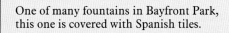

Spanish Tile Fountain, Bayfront Park, Miami, Florida 30

R. E. SIMPSON

One of many fountains in Bayfront Park,
this one is covered with Spanish tiles.

Night Scene of Band Shell in Bayfront Park, Miami, Florida   375

A closer look at the Bandshell reveals Moroccan decoration and design.

A crowd gathers to listen to a concert at the Bandshell.

Municipal Auditorium Located in Beautiful Bayfront Park, Miami, Florida   552

The Municipal Auditorium also played host to cultural events held at Bayfront Park.

The redesigned Bandshell, circa 1953.

M-13—The Bandshell in Tropical Bayfront Park
Miami, Fla.

1C-H794

ARCHITECTURE

D. C. 241—Ocean Front Hotels from Indian Creek, Miami Beach, Fla.

Ocean front hotels as seen from Indian Creek.

HOTEL ALCAZAR   MIAMI, FLORIDA

The Hotel Alcazar, at Biscayne Boulevard at 5th Street, had 250 rooms and was advertised as being 100 percent fireproof.

ALHAMBRA HOTEL — 119 S. E. 2ND STREET — MIAMI, FLORIDA

Two Blocks from Center of Shopping and Theatre District

The Alhambra, "A Modern High Class Family Hotel in a Quiet Neighborhood … Overlooking Biscayne Bay" at 119 S.E. 2nd Street.

ATLANTIC TOWERS HOTEL
MIAMI BEACH
FLORIDA

The Atlantic Towers Hotel, 4201 Collins Avenue, offered customers elevator service to the rooftop garden, a solarium, and a private beach.

Hotel Bancroft
"THE OCEAN AT OUR DOOR"

All of the rooms in the Hotel Bancroft, Collins Avenue at 15th Street, had windows with a view. The hotel also boasted a private beach, a solarium, spacious terraces, and a patio in its "European plan."

The Cadillac Hotel located directly on the ocean between 39th and 40th Streets.

The Corsair, on the ocean at 1st Street, every room had a private bath and a shower.

At the Dallas Park Hotel, on the corner of Southeast 1st Avenue and Southeast 3rd Street, "Every Appointment [was] designed to meet the requirements of a discriminating clientele."

Delmonico Hotel   Miami Beach, Florida

The Delmonico Hotel, "Completely Air Conditioned," at 64th Street on Collins Avenue.

M-182—Fabulous Fontainebleau Hotel
Miami Beach, Florida

The "Fabulous" Fontainebleau Hotel.

The Hotel Gaylord, at 2700 Collins Avenue, was complete with a "Beautifully equipped solarium and sun deck."

HOTEL GAYLORD

MIAMI BEACH, FLORIDA

SOLARIUM

GAYLORD

OVERLOOKING OCEAN

HOTEL GOOD COLLINS AVE. AT 43RD ST. MIAMI BEACH, FLORIDA

ON THE OCEAN

7A-H1878

The Hotel Good, at Collins Avenue and 43rd, claimed that it had the "Most Beautiful and Unique Dining Room in Greater Miami."

Gralyn Hotel at the entrance to Dallas Park was convenient to Bayfront Park, the theatres, churches, and downtown points of interest.

GRALYN HOTEL MIAMI, FLORIDA

AT ENTRANCE OF DALLAS PARK

8A-H3290

The Grossinger, one of the "exclusive" hotels on Collins Avenue.

The **GROSSINGER** Beach Hotel Miami Beach, Florida

The Marine Terrace Hotel, oceanfront at 27th Street, catered to "Strictly Gentile Clientele."

THE MARINE TERRACE HOTEL   MIAMI BEACH, FLORIDA

DIRECTLY ON THE OCEAN — PRIVATE BEACH   9A-H2305

One hundred of the 200 rooms in the
Colonial Hotel, facing Bayfront Park, were
air-conditioned.

"The McAllister offers every modern accommodation and
convenience. All rooms have combination bath and shower."
Located at Biscayne Boulevard and Flagler Street.

Modern hotels like the Nautilus offered their guests modern conveniences, like air-conditioning, radios, and, eventually, television.

Ultra Modern Hotels, Miami Beach, Florida

288

nautilus

SHORE CLUB

HOTEL NETHERLAND
Pool and Sundeck Club
On the Ocean
MIAMI BEACH, FLORIDA

SOLARIUM

Guests got "The Ultimate in Hotel Comfort and Friendliness" at the Hotel Netherland, oceanfront at 14th Street.

The Pancoast Hotel features Mediterranean style architecture that is common in Miami Beach.

The Park Lane Apartment Hotel at 10th Street offered "Complete Hotel Service catering to a discriminating clientele."

PARK LANE APARTMENT HOTEL   MIAMI BEACH, FLORIDA

7A-H3038

Hotel Patricia, 312 S.E. 2nd Avenue, offered "Eight Floors of Solid Comfort."

Some hotels like the Pontiac also owned apartments to accommodate guests who were wealthy or who were planning on staying longer than a few days.

RENDALE HOTEL   MIAMI BEACH, FLORIDA

BEAUTIFUL SWIMMING POOL AND PATIO

RONEY PLAZA HOTEL ON THE ATLANTIC, MIAMI BEACH, FLORIDA

The Tower of the Roney Plaza Hotel, was modeled after the spire of the Giralda Cathedral in Seville, Spain.

In addition to the hotels themselves, postcards sometimes featured attributes the hotel wished to promote. In this case, the swimming pool and patio at the Rendale Hotel, Collins Avenue at 32nd Street.

The swimming pool and cabana at the Roney Plaza Hotel.

SAVOY PLAZA HOTEL

MIAMI BEACH, FLORIDA

DIRECTLY ON THE OCEAN

A single room at the Savoy Plaza Hotel, 5th Street and Ocean Drive, cost as little as $3-$5 a day for mid-century guests.

SIMONE HOTEL.

321 OCEAN DRIVE. MIAMI BEACH. FLA.

ON OCEAN FRONT WITH PRIVATE BEACH

The Simone Hotel, at 321 Ocean Drive, had private baths, a shower, and a phone in every room in the late 1940s.

44

SOMERSET HOTEL   MIAMI BEACH, FLORIDA

DIRECTLY on the Atlantic Ocean   11 AT 1425

Guests at the Somerset Hotel at 4th Street and Ocean Drive were able to dine in their bathing suits in the hotel's Beach Front Dining Room. In 1949, a room was advertised at $1.00 and up per day per person. Five dollars reserved your room.

The cabana, pool, and private beach at The Sovereign, Collins Avenue at 44th Street.

THE Sovereign

Not only were the rooms at the Hotel Stanton, on the ocean at 2nd Street, advertised as being fairly large, they were also exceptionally "cheerful."

The Surfcomber and Seacomber hotels at 17th Street claimed that they had "Every Facility for a Perfect Vacation."

THE TATEM HOTEL MIAMI BEACH, FLA. THE TATEM SURF CLUB

A guest prepares to take the plunge off the high board at the Tatem Surf and Cabana Club at 4343 Collins Avenue.

THE VANDERBILT
MIAMI BEACH, FLORIDA

On the Ocean

Like nearly all of the hotels on Collins Avenue, the Vanderbilt between 20th and 21st Streets advertised private beach access.

Tourists in the early 1940s stroll along the promenade between the beachfront and the Wofford Hotel.

Guests went to the Suburban Club, 1519-39 N.E. 121st Street, to experience "Florida Living at its Finest."

Government Buildings

New City Auditorium, Miami Beach, Florida

280

The New City Auditorium in Miami Beach, Florida.

Built in a neo-classical style in 1914, the Federal Building and Post Office of Miami resembles many government buildings built during that time period.

209 United States Post Office, Miami Beach, Florida   10929

The Post Office in Miami Beach, designed in Federal Deco style in 1939 by Howard L. Cheney.

The Dade County Courthouse was finished in 1928 and at the time was the tallest building in the South.

Built to guide ships into Biscayne Bay, the Cape Florida Lighthouse now serves as a tourist attraction. Biscayne National Park, the largest marine park in the United States, protects and preserves a marine ecosystem that includes living coral reefs, mangrove shorelines, a shallow bay, and undeveloped islands.

Churches

The White Temple Methodist Church is one of the approximately 192 churches located in Miami.

Trinity Methodist Church, Miami, Fla.

The White Temple, Miami, Fla.

Methodists are just one of the thirty Christian denominations in Miami.

St. Patrick's Church is one of the many churches and other public buildings built in the Mission Style in Miami and Miami Beach.

The Plymouth Congregational Church in Coconut Grove was built in 1917 from oolitic limestone, which is found in Florida.

SEVEN SEAS RESTAURANT
MIAMI, FLORIDA
S.E. Cor. Southeast 1st Street & 2nd Avenue

The 7 Seas Restaurant, built in 1913 by Jerry Galatis.

THE TERRACE RESTAURANT   OPPOSITE RONEY PLAZA   MIAMI BEACH, FLA.

Completely enclosed in glass, the Terrace Restaurant is the "largest establishment of its kind in the South," facing Lake Pancoast.

53

Park Avenue
★ Restaurant

EXCELLENT FOOD · DELIGHTFUL MUSIC · SOPHISTICATED ENTERTAINMENT ·

★ club
★ bar ★ lounge

22ND STREET AND PARK AVENUE, MIAMI, BEACH, FLA.

"A visit to Miami Beach […] is Never Complete Until You Dine At" the Park Avenue Restaurant.

Wolfie's Restaurant and Sandwich Shop at Lincoln Road and Collins Avenue.

CUB DINING ROOM

Wolfie's
RESTAURANT AND SANDWICH SHOP, MIAMI BEACH

The menu at The Lighthouse featured seafood delicacies like soft shell crabs, Maine Lobster, red snapper, and green turtle steak.

EDITH & FRITZ RESTAURANT, 3236 NORTH MIAMI AVE., MIAMI 37, FLORIDA

At the Edith & Fritz Restaurant at 3236 North Miami Avenue, tourists could have all the broiled lobster or steamed shrimp they could eat for $2.

The Mayflower Restaurant, home of the Mayflower Doughnut, offered drive-in curb service.

Private Homes

D. C. 28—A Modernistic Florida Home
at Miami Beach

An example of Miami Modern style architecture that became popular after WWII.

D. C. 122—A Villa on Miami Beach

A beautiful reflecting pool welcomes visitors to this Mediterranean style villa.

D296:—A WATERFRONT HOME. MIAMI BEACH. FLORIDA

A Mediterranean villa on the waterfront.

A BEAUTIFUL MIAMI HOME. MIAMI, FLORIDA 26

PHOTO BY MANLEY BROWER STUDIO

A TYPICAL HOME. MIAMI BEACH, FLORIDA 31

PHOTO BY MANLEY BROWER STUDIO

Many of the homes in Miami, Miami Beach, and other parts of Florida reflect styles imported from the south of Spain and other parts of the Mediterranean.

D12:-A LOVELY HOME IN MIAMI BEACH, FLORIDA

A lovely looking home framed by palm trees and covered with flowers.

Patio furniture sits outside a Miami Beach estate, a place for owners and friends to sit outside and enjoy the balmy Florida weather.

Private Estate at Miami Beach, Florida   75

205   *Beautiful Entrance to Estate, Miami Beach, Florida*   11927

Red and yellow flowers form an arch over the gate to a Miami Beach Estate.

D222:-BEAUTIFUL SPANISH ENTRANCE TO A MIAMI BEACH HOME

Elaborate curves like these are very common in Spanish style decorative ironwork.

A typical Miami home with tropical flowers and coconut palms in the front yard.

Iron gates open wide in welcome at the entrance to this Florida home.

The Villa Vizcaya was built in 1916 by James Deering and employed ten percent of the city's population in the construction.

RECREATION

Smiling bathing beauties send greetings from Florida, the "Land o' Sand."

Pretty maids all in a row.

Study in Knees at Cypress Gardens in Beautiful Florida 159

A girl compares her knees to the knees of a cypress tree.

Girls in bright colored bathing suits hang in a tree like flowers.

Peaches Grown on the Beach of Miami Beach, Florida

453

A girl on the beach shares space with a Busy Person's Correspondence Card.

Bathing beauties pause for a moment before going for a swim.

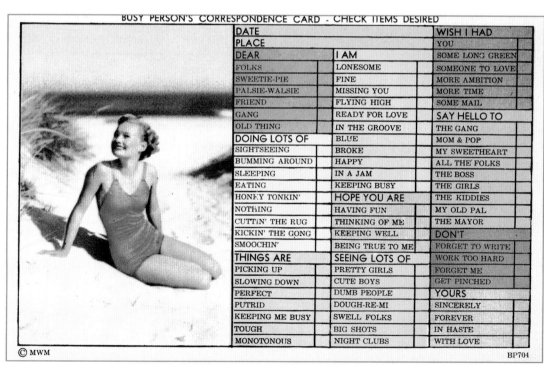

BUSY PERSON'S CORRESPONDENCE CARD - CHECK ITEMS DESIRED

		WISH I HAD
DATE		
PLACE		YOU
DEAR	I AM	SOME LONG GREEN
FOLKS	LONESOME	SOMEONE TO LOVE
SWEETIE-PIE	FINE	MORE AMBITION
PALSIE-WALSIE	MISSING YOU	MORE TIME
FRIEND	FLYING HIGH	SOME MAIL
GANG	READY FOR LOVE	SAY HELLO TO
OLD THING	IN THE GROOVE	THE GANG
DOING LOTS OF	BLUE	MOM & POP
SIGHTSEEING	BROKE	MY SWEETHEART
BUMMING AROUND	HAPPY	ALL THE FOLKS
SLEEPING	IN A JAM	THE BOSS
EATING	KEEPING BUSY	THE GIRLS
HONKY TONKIN'	HOPE YOU ARE	THE KIDDIES
NOTHING	HAVING FUN	MY OLD PAL
CUTTIN' THE RUG	THINKING OF ME	THE MAYOR
KICKIN' THE GONG	KEEPING WELL	DON'T
SMOOCHIN'	BEING TRUE TO ME	FORGET TO WRITE
THINGS ARE	SEEING LOTS OF	WORK TOO HARD
PICKING UP	PRETTY GIRLS	FORGET ME
SLOWING DOWN	CUTE BOYS	GET PINCHED
PERFECT	DUMB PEOPLE	YOURS
PUTRID	DOUGH-RE-MI	SINCERELY
KEEPING ME BUSY	SWELL FOLKS	FOREVER
TOUGH	BIG SHOTS	IN HASTE
MONOTONOUS	NIGHT CLUBS	WITH LOVE

© MWM

BP704

Pin-up shots like these, enjoyed around the world, often got their start before a camera on Miami Beach. Today models still flock to the city for the famous photo shoots that take place almost daily.

© AB504

© AB501

© AB514

M.70—Sun and Surf Bathing at Haulover Beach
Miami Beach, Florida

2C-H711

Tourists enjoy the sun and the ocean at Haulover Beach.

D. C. 55—"Sun-Time" at Miami Beach, Fla.

A typical scene in Miami Beach: sun, surf, sand, and tourists.

M-231   ENJOYING MID-WINTER BATHING AND SUNSHINE AT MIAMI BEACH, FLA.

PHOTO BY G. W. ROMER

3A-H567

TEMPERATURE TODAY IS _____°

Because Florida's climate is so mild, tourists are able to visit the beach all year.

D. C. 247—Year 'Round Bathing at 71st Street and Collins Ave., Miami Beach, Fla.

6B-H666

Beach bathers retreat from the sun beneath palm trees at the beach on 71st Street and Collins Avenue.

31 Matheson Hammoch Beach at Coconut Grove, Miami

Verne O. Williams

14965

Matheson Hammoch Beach in Coconut Grove, one of Miami's oldest landmarks.

A life of ease underneath the coconut trees.

M.72—Life of Ease Under Swaying Palms
Crandon Park Beach, Miami, Florida

2C-H713

37 TAHITI BEACH.　　　COCONUT GROVE. MIAMI, FLORIDA

PHOTO BY MANLEY BROWER STUDIO

Tahitian huts make this Coconut Grove beach look like it belongs in the South Seas instead of Florida.

Promenade at Roney Plaza Pools. 318
Miami Beach, Florida

Photo by Romer

The Promenade behind the Roney Plaza Hotel. The Roney Plaza was one of the best known hotels in Miami Beach.

Miami Beach tourists sit back and relax at a cabana.

D. C. 64—Enjoying the Cabana Life at Miami Beach, Fla.

Pool and Cabana Club, Miami Beach, Florida   286

Tourists tired of the beach take a fresh-water break beside a hotel pool.

68:—SIDEWALK CAFE AND CABANA CLUB. MIAMI BEACH, FLA.

Visitors stroll down a promenade, relax at a cabana club, or get a cold drink at a sidewalk café.

70

Macfadden-Deauville Pool, Miami Beach, Florida

365

A crowd gathers to watch a water carnival hosted at the Deauville Pool in Miami Beach.

PHOTO CITY OF MIAMI NEWS BUREAU

DC-167—Glamorous Resort Life
Miami Beach, Fla.

8B-H738

Well-to-do tourists enjoy the glamorous lifestyle offered at a Miami Beach resort.

An aerial view of the Miami Beach Dog Track.

The entrance to the West Flagler Kennel Club.

Greyhounds are paraded before spectators on their way to the post.

Nightly Gathering, Miami's Greyhound Racing, West Flagler Kennel Club, Miami, Florida

Greyhound racing fans gather in the steam-heated stands of the West Flagler Kennel Club.

73

Greyhound Parade Before Fans Prior to the Start of a Race at
West Flagler Kennel Club, Miami, Florida
434

Spectators pick their favorites before the start of the race at the West Flagler Kennel Club.

Greyhounds leap out of the starting box, also called "The Break."

"The Break", West Flagler Kennel Club, Miami, Florida

MIAMI FLA.
WEST FLAGLER
KENNEL CLUB

M-61 "BREAKING FROM BOX"

GREYHOUND RACING IN FLORIDA

AT MIAMI BEACH KENNEL CLUB

7A-H1337

When they are racing, greyhounds are muzzled to keep them from nipping the other dogs.

The World's Fastest Greyhounds Race at West Flagler Kennel Club, Miami, Florida

433

Greyhounds pursue a mechanical bunny around the track. Queen Elizabeth I of England was the first to establish the rules of greyhound racing and, in 1912, the first mechanical lure was developed by Owen Patrick Smith.

DL-26   The Flamingos at Sunset, Hialeah Park, Miami, Fla.

The flamingos that live on an island in the middle of the Hialeah Park race track. These flamingoes were imported from Cuba and South America in 1939.

D18:-

TODAY'S "LONG SHOT" AT MIAMI

A "long shot" at a Miami race track.

A view of the stands in the Gulfstream Park racecourse from the first turn of the track.

View of first turn of track with crowds in stands at Gulfstream Park Race Course
Hallendale near Hollywood, Fla.
F85

M5—View of the Walking Ring, Hialeah Race Course
Miami, Florida

Horses are paraded around the walking ring at Hialeah Park.

D. C. 258—Rear View of the Grandstand, Hialeah Park, Hialeah, Fla.

Crowds of spectators line up to enter the Hialeah Park grandstands for the start of another exciting race.

Bettors come to cash their tickets and collect their winnings after a race.

Cashing Winning Tickets at Hialeah Park, Miami, Florida 329

TOTALISATOR BOARD AND VIEW
OF THE PADDOCK. MIAMI JOCKEY CLUB
HIALEAH PARK, MIAMI, FLORIDA   40

PHOTO BY R. E. SIMPSON

Racing spectators take a breather between races
or wander over to the totalisator board to check
the odds on their favorites.

D. C. 107—Widener Fountain
and Club House Lawn
Hialeah Race Course

The fountain on the lawn outside the
Clubhouse at Hialeah Park was dedicated to
Joseph E. Widener, an important promoter
of the racecourse.

Tall palm trees line the path to the Main Club terrace entrance of the Gulfstream Park race course.

DC-270—Gulfstream Park
from Main Club Terrace Entrance,
between Miami and Hollywood, Fla.

D133:-PARADING TO THE POST
HIALEAH PARK MIAMI, FLORIDA

Horses and their jockeys parade to the post at Hialeah Park. This allows spectators to see how a horse walks and behaves before the race.

READY FOR THE RACE, HIALEAH PARK: MIAMI, FLORIDA   89

PHOTO BY R E SIMPSON

D.C.121—Horses Parading before a Race, Hialeah Park, Miami

The race participants parade from the paddock to the track, giving spectators a final look before the start of the race.

The clubhouse and grandstand at the Miami Jockey Club, one of "America's Most Beautiful Race Courses."

"And they're off!" Horses break from the starting post.

"On the Backstretch," Hialeah Park, Miami, Fla. 7

Number 3 pulls ahead on the backstretch of the Hialeah Track.

The pari-mutuel board (in the background) was developed in France around 1908 in order to help prevent cheating.

634 A FAVORITE ROMPING HOME AT HIALEAH PARK, MIAMI, FLA.

Horses thunder home for a close finish at
Hialeah Park. The invention of the photo-finish
camera made the final call much more accurate.

On the Home Stretch at Hialeah Park Race Track at Miami, Florida   95

While it experienced a decline due to rationing
during World War II, horseracing became widely
popular following the end of that conflict.

RUNNING ON THE TURF, HIALEAH PARK, MIAMI, FLORIDA—KM322

The thoroughbred horse's long legs are ideally suited for racing over flat terrain.

D. C. 103—Mid-Season at Hialeah Park

Once known as the "Sport of Kings," fans dressed up to go to the horse races, here shown at railside tables in 1945.

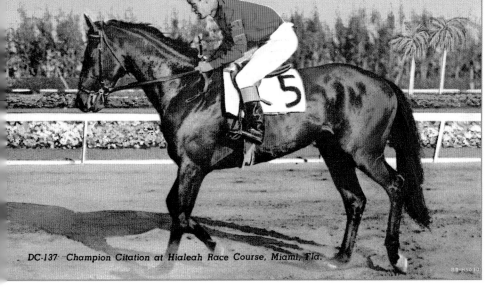

DC-137 Champion Citation at Hialeah Race Course, Miami, Fla.

A close up of a racehorse. The breed used exclusively in horseracing is the American thoroughbred. An individual horse must have extensive documentation on its background in order to be able to race.

85

At the End of a
Salt Water Fishing Trip in Florida

SEA BISCUIT

A band of fishermen relax in front of their catch of the day, circa 1950.

Home of the "Million Dollar" Fishing Fleet,
Miami, Florida   336

Miami, Florida boasts one of the finest sport fishing fleets in the world.

Many tourists come to Miami in order
to go on deep-sea fishing trips.

Deep-Sea Fishing off the Florida Coast, at Miami Beach

FLORIDA

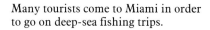

Three fairly large sailfish that were caught in the Gulf Stream off the coast of Miami, circa 1930.

A few Miamians drop a line off of County Causeway.

FISHING ON COUNTY CAUSEWAY. MIAMI. FLORIDA

Miami serves as an important port to sea traffic from all around the world.

A boatful of tourists bids "bon voyage" to Miami.

MERCHANTS & MINERS LINE

5A-H1024

A steamship belonging to the Merchants & Miners Line. This line offered trips to Miami from Philadelphia, Baltimore, Savannah, and Jacksonville.

S. S. Florida, passing thru channel at Miami, Florida, upon arrival from Havana, Cuba 504

The S.S. Florida arrives in Miami from Havana Cuba, circa 1950.

D284:—SAILING ON BEAUTIFUL BISCAYNE BAY, MIAMI, FLORIDA

Sailing ships glide gracefully
across the waters of Biscayne Bay.

85   SAILING BY MOONLIGHT ON BISCAYNE BAY MIAMI, FLA

Sailing along on Biscayne Bay.

Yachts off Bayfront Park, Miami, Fla.

PHOTO BY G. W. ROMER

Yachting is a popular water sport in Miami. Several races and regattas are held in Miami annually.

"Down Town," Yacht anchorage, Miami, Florida 337

Yacht dock in downtown Miami, circa 1944.

Wealthy yacht owners would often sail their yachts down to Miami, or hire someone to do so, and anchor in Biscayne Bay for the winter season.

YACHTS IN BISCAYNE BAY
MIAMI, FLORIDA 29

PHOTO BY MANLEY BROWER STUDIO

The yacht basin off of Bayfront Park.

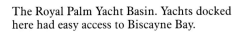

The Royal Palm Yacht Basin. Yachts docked here had easy access to Biscayne Bay.

Dade Canal and Dade Boulevard,
Miami Beach, Florida   357

The Dade Canal gave many Miami residents a place to "park" their boats and to practice water sports like aquaplaning.

Aquaplaning is similar to water-skiing except that the person being towed by the boat is standing on a board instead of skis.

D. C. 47—Aquaplaning on Biscayne Bay, Miami Fla.

M-164—Entrance to the Parrot Jungle, Red Road South Miami, Fla.

The entrance to Parrot Jungle, a zoo south of Miami where birds fly free through the park.

DC-264—Entrance to the Parrot Jungle, Red Road, Miami, Fla.

Parrot Jungle was established in 1936 by Franz Scherr, an Austrian carpenter and bird enthusiast.

A frequent stop for sightseeing tours, many of the birds exhibited there were hatched and raised on the premises.

PARROT JUNGLE, MIAMI, FLORIDA

PARROT JUNGLE MIAMI FLORIDA

The Goura-Goura, or common crowned pigeon is the largest pigeon in the world, attaining the size of a small turkey. This particular bird was hatched in Parrot Jungle.

Coral Flamingo, Rare Bird Farm, Miami, Fla   390

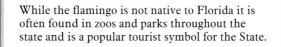

While the flamingo is not native to Florida it is often found in zoos and parks throughout the state and is a popular tourist symbol for the State.

Nesting flamingos at Hialeah Park. The first year the flamingos were introduced there, sixty-two birds were hatched.

D.C.26—Flamingos Nesting at Hialeah Park, Miami, Fla.

Flamingos share a pond with mute swans and crowned cranes.

The flamingo population at Hialeah Park was roughly 260 birds, the largest flock in captivity in the United States.

Flamingos and other exotic birds share a wading pool at the Rare Bird Farm near Miami.

Pink flamingos gaze at their reflections in a wading pool at Parrot Jungle. Flamingos acquire their pink color from the kind of shrimp they eat.

Parrot Jungle is home to several varieties of tropical parrots like these macaws and this cockatoo.

The birds at Parrot Jungle were accustomed to handling and would frequently perch on visitors.

DC-86—Parrot Jungle, Red Road, Miami, Fla.

A smiling model poses while balancing four macaws on her arm. Pretty girls were often used to advertise Florida attractions.

D224—MACAWS IN PARROT JUNGLE, MIAMI, FLORIDA

DC-87—The Parrot Jungle Red Road, Miami, Fla.

PHOTO BY CHAS. C. EBBETS

DC-266 Parrot Jungle, Red Road, Miami, Fla.

Visitors to parrot jungle were encouraged to bring their cameras to take pictures of the birds and to take pictures of themselves with the birds.

"Monkey Jungle," 22 Miles South of Miami, Florida 232

Monkey Jungle operated along the same lines as Parrot Jungle. The monkeys were allowed to roam free throughout the park.

A Hungry Alligator in Florida 172

Another of Florida's famous inhabitants, the American Alligator.

"DROP IN ANY TIME" in FLORIDA"

To prevent excess hunting and poaching, alligators are raised on farms for their leather and their meat.

M-257   LUNCH TIME AT AN ALLIGATOR FARM IN FLORIDA

PHOTO: HAMILTON WRIGHT

DL-82—Giant Galapagos Tortoises at North Miami Zoo, Miami, Fla.

The world's largest colony of the endangered Galapagos tortoise was owned by the New York Zoological Society and kept in the North Miami Zoo, circa 1940.

Twenty miles from Miami visitors could stop at Naranja, Florida to view such interesting roadside attractions as The Sausage Tree, the Plighting Rock, and the Aztec Indian Wishing Well.

WISHING WELL and Sausage TREE

PLEASE DO NOT TOUCH SAUSAGES

Clasp Hands thru this rock for Undying Love

AZTEC IND. WISHING WELL

PLIGHTING ROCK CLASP HANDS THRU THE ROCK FOR UNDYING LOVE

Wishing Well, Sausage Tree, Naranja, Fla.
(20 miles so. of Miami)   388

A SEMINOLE INDIAN VILLAGE IN THE FLORIDA EVERGLADES

SCENE ALONG THE TAMIAMI TRAIL NEAR MIAMI

PHOTO BY CHARLES C. EBBETS

A Seminole Village in the Florida Everglades, circa 1950. The Seminoles were originally members of the Creek Nation who migrated to Florida from Georgia.

What would a trip to Florida be without a round or two of golf? Once again the warm climate meant that the courses were open year round.

D25:-MIAMI BEACH, FLORIDA IS A GOLFER'S PARADISE.

Photo by Romer

45175

Night Blooming Cereus, Miami, Florida   50

The flowers that the Night-Blooming Cereus produces only last for one night.

Florida Hibiscus, Miami, Florida   419

Hibiscus are intolerant to frost, so the tropical climate of South Florida suits them ideally.

The Flame Vine and Bougainvillea, Miami, Florida   344

The Flame Vine and the Bougainvillea are two shrubs that are widely grown in Miami for the beautifully colored flowers they produce.

Originally from Madagascar, the Traveler's palm stores water in its stalks, which are beneficial to thirsty travelers.

Avenue of Australian Pines and Hibiscus in Florida

An avenue lined with alternating Australian Pine trees and Hibiscus bushes.

A Cocoanut Tree in Florida

Coconut palms are widely cultivated in Miami and throughout southern Florida.

D.C.116—The Golden Shower Tree, Miami, Fla.

The Golden Shower tree is native to the East Indies, but is also grown in South Florida. It derives its name from the "shower" of bright yellow blossoms it produces each June.

Date palms (left) do not produce fruit until they are fully grown. They are cultivated for primarily ornamental purposes and like the Royal Poinciana tree (right) can only be grown in frost free climates.

320

Royal Poinciana and Date Palm Trees, So. Miami Avenue, Miami, Florida
Photo by Romer

D. C. 130—Jacaranda Tree (Acutifolia) in Full Bloom, Miami, Florida

The Jacaranda tree creates a stunning display.

THE SAUSAGE TREE (KIGELIA PINNATA), MIAMI, FLORIDA KM331

The Sausage Tree receives it name from the oddly shaped fruit that it produces.

The Mocking Bird, the state bird of Florida shown with a branch of Orange Blossoms the state flower of Florida.

Many Miami tourists sent boxes of Florida oranges home. Others just sent a picture. Spanish settlers first brought oranges to Florida in the 16th Century.

Flame Vines line one side of a road running through an orange grove.

6A-H2161

What amazes many visitors to Florida is the fact that orange tress produce flowers and fruit at the same time.

Grapefruit and Blossoms, Florida

A Cluster of Oranges, Florida

6A-H2163

The sweet orange and the sour orange are two types grown in Florida.

Grapefruit is also widely cultivated in South Florida.

839 PICKING ORANGES IN FLORIDA

3A-H990

Orange pickers need ladders since orange trees can reach heights of up to thirty feet.

PRETTY PICKIN' IN FLORIDA G523

Orange Picking Time in Florida

Pretty women pose with the harvest, picture-perfect spokespersons for the state.

A Note About the Images

The postcards that illustrate this book are but a sampling of the many thousands produced about Miami and Miami Beach for an avid buying and collecting public. They were selected from among those available, depicting Miami at the turn of the century and on through the present day, and further culled to represent only those produced between 1930 and the late 1950s – the Linen Era.

So-named for the high rag content in the card itself, linens are very popular collectibles today. Their linen-like finish makes them a textural delight, and the gaudy dyes used in the printing process make them visual ticklers. Linen postcard production was considerably less expensive than the mainly-German produced cards that preceded it. With cheaper costs, and eye-catching colors, it was only natural that businesses began to commission cards to help advertise their services. Thus we have many hotel, restaurant, and other roadside attractions memorialized in this attractive format.

Besides their wonderful graphic value, postcards often recorded important historical events and, as in this case, preserved the look, feel, and the landmarks of an era. This fantastic collection of cards portrays important Art Deco buildings, many of which have succumbed to the ravages of time and the advances of more modern development. Linen postcard production gradually gave way to the photochrome cards, which were introduced in 1945 and predominate on the market today.

Bibliography

Capitman, Barbara Baer. *Deco Delights: Preserving the Beauty and Joy of Miami Beach Architecture.* E. P. Dutton, New York, 1988.

Cerwinske, Laura. *Tropical Deco: The Architecture and Design of Old Miami Beach.* Rizzoli International Publication, Inc. New York, 1981.

George, Paul S. Ph.D. *"Miami: One Hundred Years of History."* South Florida History Magazine v.24 no. 2, Summer 1996. Historical Museum of Southern Florida. 7/08/04. http://www.historical-museum.org/history/sfhm242htm.

Williams, Linda K. *"South Florida: A Brief History."* rev. June 1995, Paul S. George, Ph.D. Historical Museum of Southern Florida. 7/15/04. http://www.historical-museum.org/history/southfla.htm.

MORE SCHIFFER TITLES

Florida Kitsch. Myra & Eric Outwater. Florida is the land of pink flamingos, bathing beauties, palm trees, coconuts, and beaches. It is a tourist mecca and a treasure trove of souvenirs. This book is a salute to the popular Florida tourist culture of the 1940s through the 1970s, when mostly northern tourists embraced the Florida sun and beaches with open arms, discovering along with Florida's natural beauty, a lot of kooky kitsch. Kitsch is colorful, funky, fun, and collectible. This book, with its 250 photos, remembers the nostalgic, whimsical objects often bought on impulse, brought home as gifts or mementos, and visible reminders of happy trips. Whether a native of Florida, a seasonal visitor, or one in need of a getaway, this book is sure to evoke a bit of Florida sunshine for all.

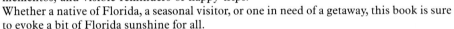

Size: 11" x 8 1/2"	247 color photos	112pp.
ISBN: 0-7643-0944-7	soft cover	$19.95

South Beach Deco: Step by Step. Iris Chase, Susan Russell, Photographer. Not just another pretty coffee table book, this information packed reference work will help you define South Beach, Florida. It is a step-by-step guide to this unique architectural and cultural wonder. Besides a variety of walking tours of the Art Deco architecture, this rich guidebook offers insight into the tempo, culture, and the habits of some very unusual daily (and nightly) South Beach customs. Whether you're a visitor, a resident, or thinking of moving here, this rich resource will provide need-to know information, from the definition of "Art Deco," to where to sip your morning coffee. Nearly 200 vibrant and artful photographs will take you on a journey filled with the romance and color of tropical Art Deco; the text will help you uncover the heart and soul of South Beach.

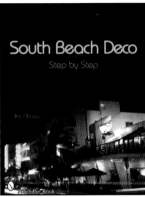

Size: 8-1/2" x 11"	193 photos	128pp.
ISBN: 0-7643-2190-0	soft cover	$24.95

South Beach Architectural Photographs: Art Deco to Contemporary. Paul Clemence with Foreword by Michael Hughes. Take a striking journey with photographer Paul Clemence through Miami's South Beach, home to some of the world's most extraordinary Art Deco architecture. Highlighting the elements that create and define the Art Deco style, these 64 black-and-white photographs capture the emotion and express the spirit of South Beach. A cross between a fine art photography and a travel book, this collection establishes South Beach's stunning visual identity, showcasing the city's landmark hotels, residential buildings, and dazzling cityscapes. A foreword written by local historian and tour guide Michael Hughes gives insight into the development of South Beach from its early days as a mangrove swamp to its current trend-setting status and the role that Art Deco architecture has played in the city's renewal. Statements from active community members paint a vivid picture of daily life in the city and give readers an understanding of the city's emotional role in the lives of its residents. This book is the perfect souvenir, and a must-have for lovers of South Beach, Art Deco, and fine art.

Size: 11" x 8 1/2"	64 b/w photos	98pp.
ISBN: 0-7643-2086-6	hard cover	$24.95

The Original Pink Flamingos: Splendor on the Grass. Don Featherstone. Text by Tom Herzing. In 1957, Don Featherstone sculptured the first three-dimensional pink plastic flamingo, thereby making affordable bad taste accessible to the American public—from Pink Flamingos. This is the tale of a wonderful bird, named by his creator phoenicopteris ruber plasticus; a new avian species, now known to all as "Pink Plastic Flamingo." The more than one hundred pictures and the text in this volume are the result of Featherstone's request that adoring owners of the pink birds send original photographs that demonstrate their affection for phoenicopteris on its 40th birthday in 1997. An overwhelming response included such masterpieces as: "Biker Birds," "What a Pear," "The Wedding Party," "Anyone for Bridge," "Purple Passion," "Beachcombers," and the sweetly romantic "Flamingo Honeymoon." If you're a believer, or even an skeptic, take a look, see for yourself. This book is one of a kind, the documentation of American genius, homage to an icon, or, perhaps, a rare opportunity to observe a culturally tolerated symbol of taste gone awry. It's great fun!

Size: 11" x 8 1/2"	105 color photos	96pp.
ISBN: 0-7643-0963-3	soft cover	$14.95